MEDITATIONS OF THE MASTERS

Edited by Ellen Kei Hua
Drawings by Kevin Miller

THOR PUBLISHING CO.
VENTURA, CA 93001

Library of Congress Cataloging in Publication Data

Main entry under title:

Meditations of the masters.

   1. Meditations. I. Hua, Ellen Kei,
BL624.M4   291.4'3   76-47649
ISBN 0-87407-203-4

MEDITATIONS OF THE MASTERS

THOR PUBLISHING COMPANY
P. O. BOX 1782
VENTURA CA 93002   *Printed in the U.S.*

ACKNOWLEDGMENTS

The editor is grateful to the following for permission to quote from their publications:

Sri Swami Chidananda and Sri Swami Krishnananda of The Divine Life Society, P.O. Shivanandanagar, Dist. Tehri-Garhwal (Rishikesh), U.P., Himalayas, India, for reprints from Elixir Divine, Kundalini Yoga, Mind: Its Mysteries and Control, Concentration and Meditation, What Becomes of the Soul after Death, Ananda Gita, by Swami Shivananda; Light Fountain, A Guide to Noble Living, and Path to Blessedness by Swami Chidananda; and Resurgent Culture and Meditation: Its Theory and Practice by Swami Krishnananda. Swami Krishnananda's kind and most generous assistance is greatly appreciated.

Swami Paramananda and Atmananda Mataji of the Sri Sri Anandamayee Sangha for reprints from Ananda Varta, Matri Vani, Sad Vani, and Words of Sri Anandamayee Ma, published by Sri Sri Anandamayee Sangha, Bhadaini, Varanasi (Banaras), U.P., India. Atmanandaji's gracious advice and assistance are highly valued.

Swami Budhananda and the Advaita Ashrama, 5 Dehi Entally Road, Calcutta 700-014, India, for reprints from Teachings of Sri Ramakrishna (1971), by Sri Ramakrishna Paramahansa.

The Navajivan Trust, Ahmedabad 380014, India, for quotes from Pathway to God (1st edition, 1971), by Mohandas K. Gandhi.

The Lama Foundation, Box 444, San Cristobal, New Mexico 87564, for quotes from The Yellow Book (1974), by Baba Hari Dass.

Drawings are opposite pages:

We are all seekers. In our search for Truth we may take many different paths, but we can all benefit from the realizations of the sages of the past and present. They who have attained enlightenment have the key to happiness. Their message is for all; take what you can and what you wish from their words.

The contemplation of a page may provide moments of solace, a few moments of reflection. Some may find answers to questions which have troubled them. Others will discover a powerful force which may activate and guide the search for that Something Else not yet experienced in life. And some may laugh aloud. This book is for everyone.

Love is the moving principle of all forms
of fellowship. Love redeems. Love transforms.
Love purifies. Love promotes understanding.

- Swami Shivananda

Love is the basis of human understanding.
Love others.
If the love is not returned, examine yourself
to see what the trouble might be.

- Confucius

Love and service -- these are the greatest ends
of all the Vedas, all austerity, all learning and
all science.

- Narada

When you see all in the One and the One in all,
you will love and serve others as part of your
own true Self. Then you will have no selfish
motives and the Awakened Mind will bring
you peace and contentment.

Do not be resentful of the works and tribulations
which fall to you in this life. Know that they
have been given to you to further your evolution
on the Spiritual Path.

- Sri Anandamayee Ma

By doing service, heart and mind are purified --
be convinced of this! To engage in service is a
very powerful sadhana (spiritual discipline); do
not become impatient. Rather serve your people
with the utmost calm and have a kind word for
everyone.

- Sri Anandamayee Ma

The Divine Music is incessantly going on within ourselves; but the loud senses drown the Delicate Music which is unlike and infinitely superior to any we can perceive or hear with our senses.

- Mahatma Gandhi

How sad to think
that you go from forest to forest
in search of That
which is within you.

- Kabir

Once gone, a day will never return.
Therefore, one must strive
to do good in every moment.
We reach the goal of the good life
by good works.

- from the Jain scriptures

And that which fell among thorns
are they which
when they have heard the Word
go forth
and are choked with cares and riches
and pleasures of this life
and bring no fruit to perfection.

- Jesus Christ

Never think of anyone as inferior to you.
Open the inner Eye
and you will see the One Glory
shining in all creatures.

- Misri

Have a joyful nature.
Do not be easily influenced
by the opinions of others.

- Swami Shivananda

Happiness comes from within.
It cannot come from without.

- Swami Shivananda

A merry heart maketh a cheerful countenance:
but by sorrow of the heart the spirit is broken.

- Proverbs

Life in this world is chaotic, fragmentary and full of unrest. The cause of suffering is the desire to enjoy the sensual objects of this world. This desire for enjoyment is due to the ignorant belief that happiness is outside you. All desires, clinging to life, all disappointment and suffering will cease forever when you realize that all happiness is within. Within you is the ocean of bliss.

- Swami Chidananda

Tso, the Spirit of the Northern Sea said, "You cannot talk to a frog in a well about the vast sea; he is limited to his area of space. A summer insect has no knowledge of snow; it knows nothing beyond its own season. A scholar of limited views cannot be talked with about the Tao -- he is enclosed by the teaching he has received."

- *Chiu Shu*

The goal of liberation is not to escape from the world but to become enlightened, wherever we find ourselves. To experience a timeless reality we do not need to run away. For those who are no longer bound to the wheel of samsara (the circle of birth and death), life on earth is centered in the bliss of eternity. Their life is joy.

- Guru Nanak

The path of duty is close at hand,
yet we look for it afar.
Our work lies in that which is simple,
yet we seek that which is difficult.

- Mencius

Evolution is better than revolution.

- Swami Shivananda

A soft answer turneth away wrath:
but grievous words stir up anger.
A wholesome tongue is a tree of life:
but perverseness therein is a breach in the spirit.

- Buddha

Watch the small irritable impulse or thought-wave
carefully. Then it will become (easier) for you
to control anger. Take all precautions. Do not
allow it to burst out and assume a wild form...
When anger is controlled it will be transmuted into
an energy by which you can move the whole
world.

- Swami Shivananda

Friends who understand each other
speak with words sweet and strong
which emerge from their hearts
like the fragrance of orchids.

- Confucius

A solid rock is not disturbed by the wind;
even so, a wise person is not agitated
by praise or blame.

- Dhammapada

He is a great monk
who can sleep soundly
in the dark recesses of the misty mountains.

- Zen saying

Your words alone do not make you a saint
or a sinner. You carry your deeds with you
wherever you go. As you sow, so shall you reap.

- Guru Nanak

A princely person is distinguished from others
by the feelings of his heart.

- Mencius

Few there are who go to the Further Shore;
the rest only run about on the bank.

- Dhammapada

Idleness is the enemy of the soul.
Seekers of the blissful spirit
must either sing the name
or be employed in doing good acts.

- St. Francis of Assisi

Nothing is hidden.
Since ancient times
it is all as clear as daylight.

- Zen saying

All our knowledge is a remembrance of what we
have known only before we were born.

- Plato

Just as a calf finds its mother among a thousand
cows, so also an action that was performed
in a previous birth follows the doer.

- Mahabharata

Instinct is simply the remembrance of actions
in past incarnations.

- Swami Shivananda

Honor both spirit and form:
the sentiment within and the symbol without.

- Sri Ramakrishna

Let your eye look with kindness,
your tongue speak with sweetness
and your hand touch with softness.

- *Swami Shivananda*

I have seen the dawn and sunset of this world.
Free from ego-love is my heart.
I watched the flowering of the bud of Truth:
It gave out its secret and smiled
and the next day was turned to dust.

- Sarmad

On the journey through life in this world nobody remains happy. The pilgrimage to the Goal of human existence is the only path to supreme happiness. Try to tread that path which is your very own, where there is no question of pleasure and pain, the path that leads to freedom from egotism and to the highest bliss.

- Sri Anandamayee Ma

To aspire to the realization of Truth
is alone worthy of man.

- Sri Anandamayee Ma

One should not pry into the faults of others
but into one's own deeds.

- Dhammapada

And why beholdest thou the mote
that is in thy brother's eye
but perceivest not the beam
that is in thine own eye?

- Jesus Christ

Searching for the Mind
is like looking for the footprints
of birds in the sky.

- Zen saying

In this mysterious cosmos, which is more like a reverberating chamber where every little sound is loudly heard everywhere and in which there can be no such thing as privacy, every thought, however feeble it may be, announces itself spontaneously and gets recorded in the subtle realms, never gets destroyed, and is repaid in a befitting manner.

- Swami Krishnananda

Some have compared this earthly life to a temporary halting of pilgrims in an inn, which is not the destination but only a means of help in the journey.

- *Swami Krishnananda*

The pilgrim passed anxiously
through the gardens of the world.
Plucking a few flowers here and there,
he departed, despondent,
not understanding the secret of the mystery.

- *Sarmad*

Wherever there is arrogance,
there is neither faith,
nor devotion,
nor wisdom.

- Swami Shivananda

Teach this triple truth to all:

A generous heart,
kind speech,
and a life of service and compassion
are the things which renew humanity.

- Buddha

Envy is the daughter of pride
and the author of murder and revenge.

- Swami Shivananda

Jealousy is the jaundice of the mind.

- Swami Shivananda

An emotion
which is overpowering one moment
and gone the next
cannot be called Love.

- Kabir

Veiled in darkness, do you not seek a light?

- Dhammapada

When the moon's light is reflected
on the surface of the ocean,
the waves make the moon appear restless,
but in reality the moon is calm and serene.
It is the water that is restless.

- Maitreya

Long must you struggle in the water before you learn to swim. Similarly, many a struggle must you pass through before you can hope to swim on the ocean of Divine Bliss.

- Sri Ramakrishna

The Sun of pure consciousness is shining in the chambers of your heart. This spiritual Sun of suns is self-luminous. It is the Self of all beings, that transcends speech and mind. If you realize this Self, you will no more return to this world of birth and death... In truth, nobody comes and nobody goes. Atman (soul) alone exists forever. Destroy fear and Maya (delusion) through inquiry -- and rest in peace.

- Swami Shivananda

At all times gaze into the heights and keep on mounting. If you aim at what is low, you will sink down into the nether-world. Accustomed to take the even, easy road, you have almost lost the ability to aspire after the sublime. Although you are in the habit of seizing opportunities as they present themselves at every moment, you fail to use this faculty in the right direction. Make a sustained effort to aim at the highest, and if your eyes cannot always remain turned towards the sky, you can surely at least keep them fixed straight ahead. The courage to climb upwards comes through enterprise and perseverance... Courage is required in whatever one does; courage itself is power.

- Sri Anandamayee Ma

Rise by your own efforts.
Do not degrade yourself.
You can be your own friend
or your own enemy.

- Krishna, in the Bhagavad-Gita

Who knows but life be that which men call death,
and death what men call life?

- Euripides

Discern and discriminate.
Evolve and expand.
Inquire and discover.

- *Swami Shivananda*

It is the duty of every human being to look carefully within and see himself as he is and spare no pains to improve himself in body, mind and soul. He should realize the mischief wrought by injustice, wickedness, vanity and the like and do his best to fight them.

- Mahatma Gandhi

Man's duty is to awaken to true humanity and to cast aside his animal propensities; to choose what is excellent and to relinquish the merely pleasurable.

- Sri Anandamayee Ma

One must learn to find enjoyment in the Sublime -- then only does one deserve to be called a human being. The search after Truth is man's real vocation.

- Sri Anandamayee Ma

The individual has a morbid habit of unconciously asserting itself as the center of experience and considering the other contents of the universe as adjectives or subsidiary elements meant to bring satisfaction to it in some way or the other.

- *Swami Krishnananda*

Do not exchange the pearl of thy soul
for the tinsel of the world.

- Kabir

Of all the problems before me
the foremost is that my heart knows no peace.
Only the Divine Beauty can appease me
through the shower of grace.

- Nazir

One should work but not seek wealth alone.
But, if wealth is gained, it must be shared
with those in need.
Beware lest wealth close the door to life.
Riches are but means to doing good
and should not become the goal of life.

- Rig Veda

By reflecting upon the miseries which all sentient beings suffer, may you be prompted to seek deliverance therefrom through enlightenment of mind.

- from The Ten Incentives of Buddhism

The superior person is satisfied and composed;
the narrow person is full of distress.

- Confucius

The one who keeps the Tao
is not affected by praise or blame.
Knowing the truth
one is not afraid
no matter what happens.

- Lao Tzu

Like the flow of the Ganges
let thy meditation be continuous.

- Swami Shivananda

May we meditate on the Supreme Light,
from which the universe has sprung forth.
It exists in all hearts
and into It will all things return.
It is the intelligence in all beings.
It is the guiding force of all intelligence.
In It we take refuge.

- Prayer of King Bharata

Q. How should we show love to others?

A. If you have love inside, it will spread every-where. Love can't be made and shown if there is no love inside our heart. If there is love inside us we don't need to show it. It will reflect by itself around us and will light the hearts of others.

What we have to do: not to hate anyone.

- Baba Hari Dass

Human happiness comes from perfect
harmony with others.

- Chuang Tzu

Through good works, you show others the way.
Do good at all times
for you can never call back a day
to perform a good deed that was neglected.

- from the Jain scriptures

Love beautifies the giver
and elevates the receiver.

- Swami Shivananda

Love and not anger is commanded.
Anger causes strife and destruction.
One should respond to anger in others
with love and kindness.
In that way he will turn away
the anger of others.

- Proverbs

The desirable and the undesirable in life are nothing but certain consequences which logically follow the whimsical and unmethodical desires of ignorant individuals who know not their own ultimate destination. What is desirable today need not be so tomorrow, and today's painful experience may be a blessing for the future.

- Swami Krishnananda

It is desire that causes sorrow, but the will
to realize God is itself felicity.

- Sri Anandamayee Ma

To a callous heart the secret is not revealed.

- Sarmad

O people of the earth!
You can take life easily
but remember that none of you can give life.
Be merciful;
Never forget that compassion
makes the world noble and beautiful.

- Buddha

Do not be a victim of the crocodile of desires.

- Swami Shivananda

In separateness lies the world's great misery;
In compassion lies the world's true strength.

- Buddha

That which is beyond this world is without form and free from suffering. They who know it become immortal, but others suffer pain indeed.

- Svetasvatara Upanishad

A boat may stay in water
but water should not stay in the boat.
An aspirant may live in the world
but the world should not live in him.

- Sri Ramakrishna

Bathe in the water of virtues;
Apply the perfume of Truth to thy body.
Thy face shall become bright.
Many gifts shall be bestowed upon thee.

- Guru Nanak

Too eager a determination
brings one to self-righteousness.
Too weak a determination
brings one to sloth.

- Buddha

If your bonds are not broken
here and now in this earthly life,
what hope is there for deliverance in death?

- Kabir

Pleasure, pain, joy, anger, excitement and regret --
such moods are like mushrooms in humid weather;
they follow each other day and night and we do
not know from whence they sprout. Stop it now!

- Chuang Tzu

Fear, jealousy, hatred, intolerance -- all these things are emotional. They do not easily go out of the mind. If anyone does something which is not to your satisfaction, immediately you get irritated, and if someone stands before you whom you do not like, feelings of hatred come. He who is not established in equanimity becomes a constant prey to fits of temper.

- Swami Chidananda

Relative happiness, which is happiness depending on anything, must end in grief.

- Sri Anandamayee Ma

Everyone runs after happiness and enjoyment. Yet supreme happiness and bliss are always "There" and nowhere else. That which is eternal must be revealed and then the question of going in search of anything does not arise.

- Sri Anandamayee Ma

The idea of obtaining eternal happiness in heaven is a vain dream... Seek the eternal bliss in your own Atman (Soul) through meditation... Everything in space and causation is bound. The Soul is beyond all time, all space, all causation. Realize this and be ever happy.

- Swami Shivananda

Behold... this world is a gilded chariot,
pulling worldly people in its wake.
The wise ones have no attachment
for the decorations of this world.

- Buddha

If you are searching for permanence in this world,
look to the rose in bloom and the changing seasons.
The fragrance of one, the reign of the other,
are like cloud's breath and then gone.

- Sarmad

Why do desires arise in the mind?
Because of the absence of bliss.

- Swami Shivananda

O seeker!
live in the world but do not become contaminated.
When plucked from the muddy pond,
the petals of the lotus flower hold no water.
When soaring into the sky,
the wings of the sea-fowl are unaffected by water.

- Guru Nanak

Beware
lest you lose the substance
by grasping at the shadow.

- Aesop

Do not grieve in this world.
Hiding in the wilderness will not bring you relief.
The world is but a mirage.
Look; it is but a ripple in the sea.

- Sarmad

Manifest plainness,
Embrace simplicity,
Reduce selfishness,
Have few desires.

- Lao Tzu

Education is not accumulation of information but assimilation of reality by degrees.

- Swami Krishnananda

Truth itself will assist in every way
him who has gone forth in search of Truth.

- Sri Anandamayee Ma

Difficulties exist only so that you may grow strong
by overcoming them. Overcome them one by one
patiently.

If you fail ten times, do not despair; if you fail
a hundred times, do not be disheartened; if you
fail a thousand times, rise up and march on boldly.
Failures are indeed stepping stones to success.

- Swami Shivananda

He who has control over his tongue
is greater than a hero in battle.

- Swami Shivananda

The words of a man's mouth are as deep waters,
and the wellspring of wisdom as a flowing brook.

- Proverbs

If you cheat the earth,
the earth will cheat you.

Blessings rarely come in pairs;
misfortunes rarely come alone.

Good fortune cannot always be with you;
flowers do not last forever.

To have forethought is easy;
to have regret is difficult.

- Chinese proverbs

At this moment
there is nothing to do
but have a good laugh.

- from a Chinese
Zen Master

When you have faults,
do not fear to abandon them.

- Confucius

One word frees us
from all the weight and pain of life;
That word is love.

- Sophocles

All mankind is one family, one people.

- Mohammed

Remember them that are in bonds, as bound with them; and they which suffer adversity, as being yourselves also in the body.

- Epistle to the Hebrews

Benevolent persons enjoy the fruits of their wealth. Misers suffer grief from their wealth.

- Swami Shivananda

He who hears the music of the Soul
plays his part well in life.

- *Swami Shivananda*

He who enjoys objects without performing his
duty is a thief.

- *Krishna, in the*
  Bhagavad-Gita

He who requires much from himself
and little from others
will keep himself
from being the object of resentment.

- Confucius

Be patient with others
but impatient with yourself.

- Swami Shivananda

To see what is right and not to do it
is want of courage.

- Confucius

Do not wish evil to anyone.
This is non-violence in thought.

Do not speak harshly of anyone.
This is non-violence in speech.

Do not hinder anyone's work.
This is non-violence in action.

- Guru Nanak

Humility is the hallmark of even they who are about to stumble into the Ocean of Reality.

- Swami Krishnananda

Do not give way to anger.
To master emotions is greater
than to be mastered by them.
Hatred is wretched.

- Buddha

Anger breeds confusion.
To be clear-minded
you must avoid being angry.

- Krishna, in the
Bhagavad-Gita

Waste not fresh tears over old griefs.

- Euripides

To be wise before an action is wisdom.
To be wise during the course
of an action is cautiousness.
To be wise after an action is folly.

- Swami Shivananda

Those who are suffering now (should) know that
they are reaping what they have previously sown,
and by sowing good deeds now they can in future
reap a rich harvest of happiness.

- Swami Shivananda

When the sky is clear
and the wind hums in the trees
tis the heart of God revealed.

- Shinto saying

O Cup Bearer!
Offer me the nectar of Immortality.
What a place this world is.

- Nazir

The path to perfection is the recognition, by degrees, of the presence of the Infinite in every moment of the individualized process of the universe.

- Swami Krishnananda

As you can change your handwriting by constant practice, so you can change your mind pattern by constant practice of positive and constructive thoughts.

- Swami Shivananda

On hearing of heavenly things,
he who can only crawl
also longs to fly.

- Guru Nanak

The Self is sitting in the chariot of the body, the intellect is the charioteer, and the mind the reins.

The one who has no understanding and whose mind is unstable, has untamed senses, like wild horses of a charioteer.

But the one who has understanding, whose mind is steady, has the senses under control, like good horses of a charioteer.

The one who is unmindful never reaches the Goal but enters into the rounds of birth and death.

But the one who has understanding and who is mindful, reaches indeed the Goal, from whence he is not born again.

- Katha Upanishad

The foam of the bubble is the daughter of eternity.
The world is an ancient inn,
crying for a new foundation.
This house stands on age-old ruins.

- Sarmad

No religion wants you to be tied down to this earthly life. All religions have as their goal the attainment of perfection, freedom and immortality. All religions also have the same process in their essence, whatever be the difference in the ritual or ceremonial details. Real Religion wants the complete annhilation of the lower self, (the) animalistic part of man, and the progressive unfoldment of his divine nature. Thus from the very genesis, we see that the fundamental principle and the ultimate goal of all religions are the same.

- Swami Chidananda

There are subjects where reason cannot take us far and we have to accept things on faith. Faith, then, does not contradict reason but transcends it. Faith is a kind of sixth sense which works in cases which are without the purview of reason.

- Mahatma Gandhi

The ocean of bliss, the fountain of joy,
is within you.
Withdraw the senses.
Look within.

- Swami Shivananda

Feel convinced that, no matter what the state of condition you may be in, out of that very state Enlightenment may come. Never harbor the idea that you are involved in sin and evil deeds and can therefore not get anywhere. At all times and under all circumstances you must keep yourself in readiness to tread the path to the Supreme.

- Sri Anandamayee Ma

In the breeze I sought the Divine Fragrance.
In the blooming garden I looked for the Vision.
But only in the meditations of my heart
Was the Path revealed.

- Sarmad

If you chase the world it runs from you.
If you run from the world it chases you.

When a person searches pleasure in worldly things
he runs after one thing. And then he thinks there
might be more pleasure in another thing, and runs
after that. At the same time, his desire for
pleasure also increases. In this way, he becomes
like a ping pong ball. But when he stops running
after pleasure, he develops contentment.

- Baba Hari Dass

If you can make your life like a running stream that swiftly and steadily flows towards its goal without ever halting, not only will no impurity of any kind be able to accumulate within you but even other people will be cleansed by your presence. Fire flares up high into the sky yet there is a point beyond which the flame cannot retain its own nature and is converted into smoke. But the current of ceaselessly flowing water is so powerful that, undeterred by the trees and rocks without number which get in the way, rivers and streams traverse thousands of miles until they arrive at their final destination. If you want to attain to Truth, you must, as a river, keep on advancing indefatigably with great singleness of purpose.

- Sri Anandamayee Ma

The worldly-minded never come to their senses, even though they suffer and have terrible experiences. Camels are very fond of thorny shrubs. The more they eat of them, the more do their mouths bleed, yet they do not refrain from making them their food.

- Sri Ramakrishna

When (the mind) does not learn the lesson of life
by enlightened reason, it has to learn it by pain.

- Swami Krishnananda

That which frees one from sorrow
and brings real bliss is Yoga.

- Swami Chidananda

The greatest griefs
are those we cause ourselves.

- Sophocles

When we yield to discouragement
it is usually because we give too much thought
to the past and to the future.

- St. Therese of Lisieux

If you wear shoes to protect your feet,
the pebbles in the road cannot affect you.
Likewise, if you remain calm
under all conditions,
the pebbles in the road of life
cannot cause you pain.

- Narada

The One who is the Eternal, the Self,
He Himself is the pilgrim
on the path of Immortality,
He is all in all, He alone is.

- Sri Anandamayee Ma

To dwell in the joy that springs from the mind's constant occupation with things divine is man's duty. Thinking of anything other than God is what creates sorrow. Be it the repetition of a sacred name or mantra, be it meditation, worship, the perusal of sacred texts, the simple awareness of God or a like device, be it the singing of God's praises or of religious music -- all these are different modes of being in the divine Presence. One should always be engaged in one of them, in fact never be without them.

- Sri Anandamayee Ma

Blessed are they who walk the Way
aware by night and day
that life is sacred still.
They strive for Peace
and ever before them
shine the noble Truths of life.

- Buddha

May all beings be loving and kind to each other;
May all beings realize the good within;
May all beings think well of one another.

- the prayer of Prahlada

May the world be free from the fear of war
and destruction, from the delusion of fostering
civilization through enslavement, from the self-
righteous pride of charity and of doing good to
others, from ungodliness and the unhealthy dia-
lectics of materialism. May Peace be unto all
beings.

- Swami Krishnananda

Lead me from the unreal to the real.
Lead me from darkness to light.
Lead me from death to immortality.

- Brihad-Aranyaka Upanishad

GLOSSARY

Aesop (c 620-c 560 B.C.) - Greek writer of fables.

Anandamayee Ma (1896-   ) - Sri Anandamayee Ma ("bliss-filled mother") is one of India's greatest saints. She has many ashrams throughout India and followers throughout the world.

Atman - The Self, or Soul.

Baba Hari Dass - A sage from India, currently residing in the United States.

Bhagavad-Gita - India's immortal scripture (which forms part of the Mahabharata) in the form of a dialogue between the hero Arjuna and his charioteer-guru Krishna.

King Bharata - An ancient great king and religious leader of India. The name for India in Hindi is "Bharata."

Brihad-Aranyaka Upanishad - See Upanishads.

Buddha (c 566-c 480 B.C.) - Great Indian saint and founder of Buddhism.

Chiu Shu (1130-1200) - Chinese philosopher and mystic.

Chuang Tzu (4th century B.C.) - Chinese Taoist mystic and philosopher.

Chidananda, Swami - Current President of The Divine Life Society, with international headquarters in Rishikesh, Himalayas, India, and a direct disciple of Swami Shivananda, founder of the Society.

Confucius (c 551-c 478 B.C.) - Chinese philosopher and teacher. Also known as Kung Chiu.

Dhammapada - Hinayana Buddhist text, purportedly written by Buddha.

Euripides (c 480-406 B.C.) - Greek dramatist.

Francis of Assisi, Saint (c 1182-1226) - Great Catholic saint of Italy, founder of the monastic Franciscan Order.

Gandhi, Mohandas K. (1869-1948) - Hindu sage, religious leader and social reformer of India. The people of India bestowed upon him the title of "Mahatma," meaning "great soul."

Ganges - The holy river of the Hindus, which flows southeast from Gangotri in the Himalayas into the Bay of Bengal near Calcutta.

Jain(ism) - An ascetic religion founded in the 6th century B.C. in India by a Hindu reformer as a revolt against the caste system.

Kabir (1450-1518) - Hindu religious reformer and saint who had both Hindu and Moslem followers.

Katha Upanishad - See Upanishads.

Krishna (c3100 B.C.) - The beloved Avatar (divine incarnation) of India, who appears in the Bhagavad-Gita as the guru of Arjuna.

Krishnananda, Swami - Current General Secretary of The Divine Life Society, Rishikesh, Himalayas, India, and a direct disciple of Swami Shivananda.

Lao Tzu (6th century B.C.) - Chinese philosopher, reputed founder of Taoism.

Mahabharata - Ancient epic poem of India of which the Bhagavad-Gita forms part.

Maitreya - Ancient great saint of India, contributor to the Upanishads.

Mantra - A sacred syllable or formula whose vibratory potency brings the chanter to a heightened state of consciousness.

Mencius (c380-289 B.C.) - Also known as Meng Tzu. Chinese philosopher.

Misri (9th century) - Sufi saint.

Mohammed (570-632) - Arab prophet, founder of the Islam religion.

Nanak, Guru (1469-1538) - Indian religious leader and saint, founder of the Sikh religion.

Narada - An ancient great Hindu saint of India, first mentioned in the Chhandogya Upanishad and then in the Bhagavata, which relates the life of Sri Krishna.

Nazir (1735-1846) - A Sufi poet-saint of Northern India.

Prahlada - An ancient saint of India, devotee of Krishna.

Ramakrishna Paramahansa (1836-1886) - Great saint of India, founder of Ramakrishna Mission (the Vedanta Society).

Rig Veda - See Vedas.

Sadhana - Spiritual discipline; this differs according to one's individual needs and spiritual path.

Samsara - The wheel of births and deaths through which each individual soul must pass until enlightenment is attained.

Sarmad (d. 1657) - Poet-saint of India.

Shinto(ism) - Native religion of Japan, primarily a system of nature and ancestor worship.

Shivananda, Swami (1887-1963) - Hindu saint and founder of The Divine Life Society in Rishikesh, Himalayas, India. Before becoming a monk, Swami Shivananda was a practicing medical doctor for many years.

Sri - holy; a title of respect.

Sophocles (c495-c406 B.C.) - Greek philosopher and dramatist.

Svetasvatara Upanishad - See Upanishads
Tao - The Way; in Taoist philosophy, that in virtue of which all things happen or exist.

Therese of Lisieux, Saint (1873-1897) - A great Catholic saint of France. She is known as "the little flower" to her devotees.

Upanishads - In Hinduism, a class of treatises, usually in dialogue form, composed between the 8th and 6th centuries B.C., having as their principal message the unity of the soul with the Divine.

Vedas - The body of sacred Hindu scriptures, chief among which are the Rig Veda, Sama Veda, Yajur Veda, and Atharva Veda. The Vedas contain information and instruction in every field of human endeavor and have formed the basis of the Hindu religion since ancient times.

Yoga - The science whereby the individual soul is united with the Divine. There are many yogic paths but the main divisions are: Bhakti Yoga (the path of devotion), Karma Yoga (the path of right action), Jnana Yoga (the path of discrimination and wisdom), and Raja Yoga (royal or complete yoga).

Zen - A form of spiritual discipline derived from Mahayana Buddhism, introduced in the 6th century A.D. in China, and into Japan in the 12th century.